Plain Text

Plain Text

Michael Vince

Mica Press

Published in the United Kingdom in 2015

by Leslie Bell trading as Mica Press
47 Belle Vue Road, Wivenhoe, Colchester, Essex CO7 9LD
www.micapress.co.uk | books@micapress.co.uk

ISBN 978-1-869848-03-3
First Edition

Contents

Plain Text

From Herodotus

BRIDES IN THE BATH

Waterlow Road, once Bismarck Road

Usually there are flowers, tearful messages, photographs
tied to a post or bus-stop or heaped against a wall:
exercise-book pages in plastic dampen, the ink runs –

loose bunches of wind-troubled roses still wrapped
in sodden paper flop down against the binds of string.
Our local murders: brief paragraphs in the news

followed by court appearances make less impression
and vanish sooner: two boys shot outside a nightclub
just casualties in the drug wars, or the casual stabbing

of the upright man by the one who simply doesn't care –
troubled enough in their minds perhaps to be called mad
though nobody quite mentions that. Our recent murders:

those who knew about them or witnessed them might pause
at the places when remembrance has been tidied up –
but people have, as we say, moved on. So no-one

stops outside this house to look. Even the name
of the street is different now, the lodging house a valuable
suburban home. The air is cleaner, flowering trees

line the pavements, and if there are any ghosts at all
of either the hanged man in his last prison garments
or of the drowned Bride, naked, white under the water,

they have soaked into air, unrestrained by any string,
rain-blotted letters or withered stems, their faded deaths
like Whittington's London gold trodden into the pavements.

PAVEMENT ARTIST

for Ben Wilson, painting somewhere

On the dead road by Archway corner, a drunk
sprawls on the pavement before ten in the morning.
Or perhaps it's telecoms – his right hand sunk

under the pavement, though no cables trail there,
purple, green, orange: those are in his paintbox
and on his brush. I don't want to stop and peer

over his shoulder as he works, but wherever I go
I find on paving stones tiny medals of gum –
seventeenth-century icons transmuted to a glow

by a bearded miniaturist. There on the ground
they shine everywhere, little coats of arms
framing a clenched fist, the Arsenal, a crown

of flames, new images enlightening the road,
but trodden unnoticed, scuffed, chipped, fading,
or scraped by street cleaners who have not understood.

One day I stop and talk to him and ask if he'll
come to our street and paint outside our house
a mark of its familiar, our big white cat, a real

heraldic beast, deaf to the world, gentle and slow
or irritable and noisy. He carefully writes down
the address on a corner of paper but doesn't show,

but I imagine the tiny badge with a cat's face
outside our door, to blazon the painter's circulation
on the vague currents of London, and stamp the space

of the neighbourhood, under whose brick burden
in the soil, jewelled flowers ghost woods and pasture,
and sweat-stained faces shine in lost market gardens.

MASTER GAVIN DOUGLAS'S EIGHTEEN MONTHS

...hys request ane command

The Roman world, tendrils of vine, tiny
household gods, ranked legions before fall,
recede across river-boulders misted with spray,
borne on strict columns, layered brick-tile.

In the dark hours, tallow candle by fire-light,
line after line of words unlock, weighed up,
and on dour days, snow blackening in the lane,
the poem, time's aqueduct, channels their flow.

The hero bears his father on his back away
from the burning city. Great poem, favourite child,
I carry you pacing about in my turret room,
shouldering your rhythm beyond the world's limit.

Onwemmyt – unstained – is how I describe fame,
that of my master poet: small stones, some tesserae
sieved from a hill-site, the near burn scouring clean.
Eighteen months now faded in gleaming weather.

HERR MARX AT THE SEASIDE

The prevailing rush of air eats away at Boniface cliffs
for nothing is permanent, the whole human resort

sliding back into the sea. At least here he can breathe,
exhausted brain and shuffling limbs re-enlivened

by that Promethean blast. Ladies' hats can hardly resist
and weighted skirts tug like sails of wandering barks

scudding offshore and pointing at France and at failure.
One might, he considers, be a prehistoric sea-creature

whose remains will sink to the mud bottom and in time
find oneself pure, mere bone, compressed into a fossil,

and in some later age of the earth when future workmen
cut into a hill-reef of chalk, look, there you will shine

though oddly as if a shadow, an undigested silicate,
a lump in the throat or an unchallengeable argument,

those traces of the pre-diluvian world in North London
in the cutting at Archway. Time to walk back to the guest-house

for a doze, to sink into that fierce diurnal dreaming,
the Terra Incognita of the future whose edge of convulsion

is marked by this awkward ancient badly-drawn sea monster
with foul cigar and slippers and daughter dutifully attentive.

IVY

Balanced on one crutch, he pulls
the ivy down using a stick,
not easy when the stem has rooted in so much
and wound up the house wall.

Nor will he accept to be dislodged
in his eighties now.

He can't complain, he says
eyes bright as berries when he sits to talk
winding his story from the ivy stem
down to its root.

It grew up from next-door, that family
he remembers the day they came, though not sure
what year it was.

The father worked nights pasting up posters
on the Underground
and doing decorating jobs
around the neighbourhood.

Borrowed his ladders, for example.
Bring them back I told him, and he promised that he would.

One day a van appeared and the family was gone.
There'd been some disagreement there.

All that was left was ivy, thick, unyielding
as a stream of words.
No matter how you pull at it, it comes
pushing its way back.

MARVELL'S HOUSE

...being resolved now to sequester myself one whole day at Highgate...

A poet, gentlemen, learning's young personage,
must converse with masters, dead and living,
Horace and Jonson. There is always much to say,
more to learn and the gaining of value and weight –

though not of daily bread. One journeys abroad,
guide of the privileged Youth; a noble family
engages another as tutor. Verses are a road
down which deft feet go towards employment.

This is my path, I have ridden it, this is what I am.
A few miles beyond the limits of the City,
debates in the House, letters to the Corporation
of Hull, I retreat to this house on its green hill

wearied perhaps or withdrawn, as in my verses
into my Idea. You, gentlemen, may decide
the needs of your most humble servant. I gaze
from a green fringe across dust and smoke pall,

towards what I might once have conjured. The soul,
gentlemen, thus covers its face, it contemplates
far noise, harsh cries, it is silent and knows itself
less pure than once it was, world-harmed, life-tired.

Shouts of drovers and the placid lumbering
of beasts herded to their death pass near my door.
Here gentlemen, my most worthy friends, I rest
walled in my garden and quiet beside the North road.

A FOODIE, FORDIE

...Ford Madox Ford in heaven...

To cooking, like all you did, you gave complete attention,
the task in hand shutting out complication and confusion,
whether as an unlikely officer serving in the Trenches -

were you really admired by the Army and asked to sign on
as a Regular after the Armistice? - or whether as writer singly
seeking out the right word. The good food of the peasantry

was what you loved, you said, and your wildly contradictory
and untrustworthy touches, well-seasoned in the making,
can be savoured like a good meal. Similarly you admired

the exemplary life of the self-sufficient small producer
feeding off his own land after working it with the hoe,
an art learnt, you said, by studying the subject in Paris:

food for thought, as if you were the Flaubert of market-gardening.
There was marital redefinition, nerves, gassing and shell-shock
and bitterness for France betrayed and British hard-headedness,

but further off there was always a tumbled cottage with a pig
and hens and comedy retainers. Was it truly a leg of lamb
braised with shallots that you ate that night in Red Ford cottage,

your famous crisis of starting again, or was it a slice of beef
or half a chicken stewed: it hardly matters if you served up
a different dish to different readers. That's how cooking

works, adapting to ingredients, never exactly the same
twice over, for never the same taste. Mostly you could afford
small hotels and low-rent houses with home-made furniture,

but later, on the slopes of Provence, above the sea in a borrowed
paradisical villa, there were beans, squash, aubergines,
tomatoes and *fines herbes*: even, you suggest, your own wine.

The heat necessitated abstemious meals, yet you lost no weight -
it was olive oil and the *fines herbes*, you said. You were growing old,
and here you watered and wrote in your last idealised *terroir*,

old time peasant, self-sufficient, before and beyond your time.
You stand there portly in your apron waiting for curious guests
who will need a drink and some olives after their exhausting climb.

MR BONKERS

Bowed to the ground with hunched shoulders
and shiny head, a roll-up stuck on his lip,
he'd be toiling up or down hill, towards
or away from the park. On a length of clothesline
out ahead, tugged the dog, part beagle,
part any dog. That was Bonkers. Slowly,
man and dog with their umbilical cord

inched upwards. If we patted the dog
it wagged or snarled, happy and unhappy
to have schemed introductions. The man looked
down as he talked. He'd been on his own,
the dog was a gift from his son, it was a bugger
but needed a walk. Across North London,
wherever we went, Camden, Kentish Town

even some miles astray in Chalk Farm once,
there they were, stretched out, panting, wild
to sniff and stop, one bent in on himself,
like a pair of compasses measuring London
over and over, its dimensions ever inexact
but defined yard by yard along its pavements
by the extent of human and canine restlessness....

POTTERY FRAGMENTS

First, men's feet and horses, then a slanted line of swans:
beside them a woman's arm holds out a bronze mirror,
and a satyr's cut-off torso, just mid-riff cock and thighs,

lunges at someone's buttocks. While the bridegroom
seizes the veiled bride's wrist, over here men with spears
march over the edge, small isolated flowers grow,

some part of a corpse is dragged behind half a chariot.
An absent world pushes the small figures apart:
their broken pieces tear and tear at the heart.

ST ALBANS

Thank you van Ruisdael:
burgeoning shapes of clouds
borrowed by highlights in the trees
twisted frames
of tree-trunks make emblems against the sky,
urge their meaning

as driving round and down the hill
the sight of St Albans cathedral
from the M25 anticlockwise
foursquare in the sun
on an autumn evening

THE REAL

The queue straggles as far as the door and inside
we wait, two propped up on the dividers marked
DO NOT LEAN, an ancient man with crutches
waiting on a seat, kids in pushchairs, a thin boy

with a parcel, the rest of us holding letters, forms,
or packets, some hands in pockets, one in a rough
hairy suit; we sigh and watch the lined shufflers
in front, or count who's left, or listen out

for the next announcement and the number's
magical change. What we are waiting for
could be anything: justice, for example –
that takes long enough – or the final judgement

when we are weighed and found wanting,
or rewarded at last for what we never suspected
our virtues were. So many lines of people
like names in a ledger or faint lines of memory,

footsteps in the thin rain waiting by the roadside,
patient in death as they had not been in life.
A woman in front, mouth-to-phone, steps
forwards and the space she leaves closes up

and a poster declares that this is the Post Office:
if anything binds us together in our separateness
it is standing and waiting and looking at our watches
and complaining and following with or without

patience, dumbly, regretting that we came, wishing
there had been some other way of managing it
or of avoiding it completely. The very smell
on a wet day hot in here makes it The Real

though everyone here would settle for the opposite.

TRAFFIC

John Ruskin: Eagle's Nest 1872

Every increased possession
loads us with a new weariness:
a doubled up line of traffic

round the Tavern giratory,
on past the Venetian brick
grandeur of the old infirmary

eyed from its pointed towers
by a nesting sparrowhawk
scanning to see a vole stir:

it creeps along line by line,
mothers with laden school-run
four-by-fours, Serco vans

transporting prisoners, giant
lorries weighed down with steel,
supermarket ready-washed salads,

until the whole gut length
passes beneath the decorative span
of Archway Bridge at the top

of the hill, squeezes round
the curve and has idled on.
Wheels turn, we have far to go,

things to do. Drivers yawn,
sing along to the radio,
make mobile talk. Hello,

we are all fine, more or less.
Every increased possession
loads us with a new weariness.

WATER BOATMAN

There is the sky above the water, a fringe of twigs,
the neighbouring meadow and a road leading
to the city: it is the world of experience.

Then there is the water itself, solid enough
but ever in motion, even this rather dull pond,
for the wind moves across it, the spirit perhaps

over the water, and also through its pale depths
down to its chalky bed, surprisingly white,
a pale anti-world with a reflection up at the top,

an underworld with dead things at the bottom.
On the line between the two perches the water-boatman
with its legs tensed against the filmy surface

like an old man resting in time, skimming the border
between two elements, the airy past, the watery
liquid future with its terminal gleam. Man is an insect

it declares, and like those getting old it quivers
and shoots off, precarious still, balanced on nothing
face-down in the silent waters seeking nourishment.

COLONEL DESPARD

1751-1803

I was up too close in the road not named for you
and wishing that you after all might define my address,
disgruntled plotter, failed rebel. Your brother
was a more likely name-donor: an established success

of ambition and military achievement, risen at last
to fame as respected general. You marched in those footsteps
on sugar slave islands, on the lost Mosquito Coast,
sword-cut or fever-sweat, and gained your command,

married a former slave and upset all the colonists:
they contrived your downfall, your removal, your disgrace.
Slaves might be freed, it seemed, but not be made equal:
you had overstepped your beliefs, you fell out of place.

At home where talk was of uprising and assassination,
of government wrong-doing, those listening were spies.
At your trial even the words of Horatio Nelson
were not enough: you were hanged and your head struck off

on a prison roof. Your name seems much too grand
for a narrow closed-off street, one of the by-ways
of the Great North Road, though the place holds you up
like the long view South bright above the traffic haze.

AUTOBIOGRAPHICAL NOVEL

End of book: slow rooks of print wheel round
to settle in the covers. Quiet descends

on the deserted churchyard, the headstones
of Father hardly known but deeply mourned

and Mother daily lost, and childhood friends
grown into awkward men. The enemy

who spoiled all and stole and coveted
even pale innocence, pure unselfish love

above his understanding, now brought low,
is forced to make amends and well punished -

all who have suffered, the mad, the poor, the vain,
at last transformed. For some death quietly

slips them out of the narrative, for others,
the worthiest, chance grants them every comfort,

respectability or such improvement
as gives future hope. The most mistaken,

and most perhaps the author, duly gain
enlightenment, through suffering: folly

of youth if tended rightly may yet outgrow
original error and find in life some comfort,

even in the loss of the inadequate wife
so dearly loved, that mere girl so unsuited

to survival in the story. Who was it she resembled
laughing among her curls? Who was it whose

jealous guardian lap-dog would always fend off
those who read too closely? A better ending

further from truth now tends his final house,
story's end, where he makes himself at home

with a family of creatures and with fame
his housekeeper, and that unmarked page, desire.

GREY LAGOON

after Guardi, for my neighbour

The dark body of the boat, a shadow
on the grey water, the man rowing at the stern
picked out in silver.
                    All his life
they said at his death, the painter
worked for his daily living.
The years of grey unrippled water
undistinguished from the sky.
                    My neighbour
smooths his voice over the years
like his hands over slabs of wood
with measure and saw, with chisel and plane.

'I earned the wage, did all the little jobs.
Bills paid, trees grafted, roses exactly pruned:
after the day's work there was the house
to be furbished and sanded, jointed and painted.
The kitchen was hers. She liked things
to be just so.'
                    His wife now gone,
her mind gone long before,
his hands now stiffened by age
must still support him on crutches:
'Once I'm down, I can't get up.'

The silver pole of the crutch
must be pushed into the grey water.

In this last painting where sky and sea meet
the city hangs without past or future,
shining stone unearthly in mist.
He had 'procured universal approval',
Francesco, but died in poverty.

Far out in the lagoon, the boatman
leans to cross the darkening water.

Work to be done, taking him home.

LOST DAUGHTER

Three decades ago dead at birth
your name chosen but not given,
your body unseen except by those

who disposed of you: your identity
hung between a loss and a never
to be – you said no words,

sang no songs, had no scuffed knees
nor leapt into the shallows:
life of your own you failed

to grasp: how you pronounced
words childishly, spoke names
of other girls; your resemblance

to the faded photo of your aunt
gone before you; the tender
heat of holding hands. In mine

slip through fingers airy spaces
of your growing up, not disturbed
by your actual breath or by turbulent

currents of you-and-me: my dad,
you'd say, can be so annoying,
or later, we get on really well

considering: what's left unsaid,
unchangeable and of no existence
even though I feel you there.

A part of me that released you
into being urges me with words
to give you life belatedly

in lines like strings of DNA
winding across your unlived years
connecting us umbilically,

my dead girl. I give your frail
thread a tug from far off to say
hello, as if it's your birthday.

THE ORCHID GROWER'S MANUAL

Victoria and Paradise Nurseries, Upper Holloway, 1885

When I go noisily down
to the hothouse of the Northern Line
the heavy scent of orchids,

waxy flowered, pungent as vanilla,
floats there to be grasped
as if by some Victorian collector

who has sweated through rainforest
and along mist-obscured peak trails
in the insect-laden empire of time:

a fictional world, for whose uprooted
aliens, pampered and enslaved,
nursery boys tend coke-fired stoves.

Rooted above us behind glass
in the Victoria and Paradise Nurseries,
those bulbs coddled in new loam

can only ghost with late fragrance
ruined soot-darkened plant houses,
each glass frame bare and derelict,

sold off to gleam from photos taken
before the Tube was dug. Undermined
by vanishing, their perfume filters

down shafts whose busy crowd
turns heads bowed from that heavenly field of delights,
                                    a distant glow
of orchids astounding the paned sunlight.

HOUSES

The houses of the writers of London:
crammed with vagrant families
chipped and flecked and stunted by bombs

the bars above the door-light to keep thieves out
the boiler in the basement for the house skivvy
smells of cabbage and children and horse dung

The houses of the writers of London:
the beloved cat watching shadows from the sill
pure water drawn from the well in the cellar corner

and the friendly robin taking crumbs from fingers
in the enclosed garden
                    or the poets smoking in the kitchen
walls pierced with vision of the starved crouching in the street

PLAIN TEXT

It is a precious jewell to be plain

John Dowland

There is much to mourn and much that is unclear,
where the mists of Deptford ripple the mud-flats
of the Thames in passing. On this alluvium

stems of small plain plants root and nod
with cans and hoops and stumps of concrete,
and the outline of the dead railway embankment

sinks further into its forgetfulness
through the grass: boat-builders and reed-cutters
and factories which resist direct statement,

for their roofs and walls are gone, still wring hands
together where tracks of cobbled roads emerge
clearly unpacked from droplets of soot or sweat:

rain falls onto cleared sites, overgrown plots.
The ruined place encumbered here with all this
yet cuts clear. Along edges of rubbled corners

it spawns the return of its age-long cast-off flora
names plain-spoken: goatsbeard and shepherd's rod
money-wort, bugloss, cudweed, water parsnip,

there is no end to their assured possession.
Simple bells tolling, seed bells, water bells.
Plainness, wild gladness, cancelling emptiness.

RENAISSANCE YOUTH

In a small grove a figure reclines gazing outwards:
ear-ringed, doublet embroidered with starry flowers,
his head leaning on his arm, the legs extended.

The trees are a tangle of the body of the world
which extends a protective shade, or an entangling bulk
or error, they creak and sway this way and that

over the textured grass jewelled with tiny blooms.
Is that an easeful smile he shows, or mere puzzlement,
the front feature of an ambiguity? Is this the soul

unmoving, a gaze as into glass, the mind at rest,
the body balanced upon beauty quiet and still
in the summer shade? Composed here, poised

lie youth, good looks, comfort and prosperity
in a day's painted idleness, as if tomorrow's battle
might not keep gathering. Behind him, at the edge

of the tiny wood, a groom holds the head of his horse
impatient and pawing at the earth for the chase to begin,
a world intransigent, unwilling to be conquered.

THE HILL RUNNER

William Powell, the Highgate Prophet

How doth the world continue? Day to day winds blow
rain falls, trees stretch and flap, lumpy cloud strata
obscure Highgate Hill with its scintillant cobbles.

None of these owns innate inevitability. It depends
for its proceeding and being itself on a single human will,
my own. Movement drives me to maintain this fragile world,

its dependent hues, the subterfuges of sun's rays through air,
bright horse piss with its splash of odour steaming on the road,
four iron posts, a woman's clattering hob-nailed boots.

Dawn finds me setting off each day devoted to sustain it –
past the Assembly Rooms, across the stream, through the fields
intent to store the hay, to keep those sweet cuttings safe

before I reach the base of the hill. I stop here. I survey the fallen
world,
decay still tumbling down and down, O let me keep us from it.
So I begin my run, faster, panting, the heart leaping

and up the angle of the Hill, without pity. Slow labourers
pace on, ignorant of their salvation, overtaken by my rising.
My sweat runs, the pulse beats in my head, fertile brain

tending, animating the world's root-ball, tubers of blood
till I reach the top. For another day, the world is saved,
it will not end. Dark elms reach out now branches of thanks

and in grandeur, the petticoated chestnuts flaunt their candles,
a dog runs barking round me and the hill people point and laugh
not praise, nor thank, for the continuing of their world and mine.

TOYS

Listed in the census
are the seven people who lived
in our house a hundred years ago.

One was a Turkish bath attendant,
another was a groom,
and a couple, middle-aged, are described

as 'toy cannon makers'. Imagine
hurrying in the eighteen nineties
each morning to the toy factory

off Hornsey Road. All that precise
casting – the lead pourers
would suffer and die in the end –

and detailed paintbrush work:
well-dressed boys came home
and played at soldiers thanks to them,

their hours bent at the work bench.
The cannon they made are now
collectors' pieces. And the pair

who washed and ate and slept here
fade here listed and named
under layered wallpaper, distempered

shades, originals of the house,
blank leaves faintly recovered
from time's walls' palimpsest.

THE VOW

One pours the wine and kneels. Others
standing by bear witness to the vow –
'if my wish is granted then I shall give

et cetera, et cetera...' Or another
in the heat of battle pleads with the god
and promises whatever he has to give:

grant me this victory, let me live,
keep safe my son. *Voti reus*,
one whose vow must be fulfilled:

until the reckoning has been made
you live between heaven and earth,
you owe everything, you have given nothing.

Whether you must travel to the shrine
barefoot or on your knees, whether
you must offer all you have

at the foot of the altar, or whether
you merely accept that you are changed,
diminished by what you owe

but cannot give, in any case you are bound
to relive your need, your failure.
The impossibility of the vow –

that is the stumbling block
of your belief, the hardest step
you cannot refuse and cannot take.

WHITTINGTON

It was a complete pantomime. The hero,
something in the City, was hardly 'the genius
of the neighbourhood', but his wife, to be cruel,

did resemble the cat, a homeless cat,
slinking between parked cars. Seeking
one's fortune, one does not necessarily

turn again. Luck can turn on you too,
the distraction of a moment - turn again -,
a wheel buckling on ice, sheer exhaustion

at the end of a hard day - so the curtain falls
and he's gone. What's left is more of a tragedy,
friends weeping in church, crying children,

and the woman unmoved behind her mask.
The locals endowed with almshouses
shout 'Oh yes it is' or 'Oh no it isn't'

while neighbours who hardly knew him well
wish they had been by the roadside
to call 'Look out behind you'.

From Herodotus

A VISIT

What has happened to this place?
Cracked hearthstones, a dried-up well,
the line of a road pointing away –
why have I come here? There is nothing to see.

My royal foot scratches in the dust,
and I summon my librarian. The name,
he says, of this barren empty hill
was one that all men trembled at,

and its kings, rich in gold and grain
and jars of oil and armed men
ruled as far as that trembling blur
over there, the sea. Their names,

however, and the name of the place
are forgotten. A scatter of tiles,
and long-winged birds high circling
act out their ceremonial

of memory. He stares, and bows.
The place is a trap, now I understand,
as my banner droops on the hilltop.
The name is an emptiness I have brought with me.

ONE SHIP TO SALAMIS

Siphnos and Serifos sent one ship each to fight with the Greeks against the Persians at Salamis.

A mule clatters on cobbles from a hidden yard,
its rider greets us with the wave of a hand,
and we stop and sweat. Better to stay at home,
too hot for walking, he calls to us. It is hard

going, sure enough, on rough-laid stones
between crumbling walls: tiny yellow snails
gleam fresh at the edge of the path after rain.
The track heads on now, following the bones

of village mule-paths laid down before roads
up from the coast. Frogs ripple in a pool
and vanish under stones, overhead
sway the arched wings of predatory birds

buoyed on air. The path wavers on ahead:
it's the last chance we have to walk this way
before the boat leaves for home. High up
above the sea in a small empty farmstead

where sprout in sparse patches beans or oats,
penned in darkness there feeding her young
lies a great tufted sow, and a rainbow cockerel
struts, and munching in the thorns, goats

peer from the rocks. As if the land still rests
after its one great effort, that single ship
it sent to Salamis, its proud urgent crew
hunching the shape of the island in their breasts,

their amulet, these days there is not much here:
vagrant foreigners, bitter ocean wind
browsing the scrub oak, traces of the last springs
fed by winter, their overflow trickling clear

over the worn rim of this ruined stone shell,
time's empty carapace. One ship to Salamis,
the oarsmen bent into a scattering of rain,
the ship's wake's foam dissolving in the sea-swell.

THE FISH

Some awkward god directed it into the poor man's net, that fish,
so large he struggled to haul it over the side of his frail boat,
then watched its great jaws gape as it thrashed about in its throes,
its armour of scales gleaming, its eyes staring mutely

until it was still. His hands were bloodied, he wanted to sit and
                                                                   sleep.
The sea lay flat, the moonlight trapped him in the wide open
with nowhere to hide. It was the biggest fish he had ever seen.
He had raised it from the depths of another world and defeated it.

But though he had rejoiced at the thought of profit, as he wiped
his forehead with his hand, smearing it rust-red, while he drifted
round and about, uncertain of the shore, becoming overweighed
with the thought of it, and afraid of whichever god it was

who snared both man and fish, there was only one thing he could
                                                                   do:
at dawn onshore he manhandled the monster onto his cart
and headed for the palace. The fish must be a gift for the king.
The guards helped him to drag the thing along the marble corridors

to the audience chamber: the fisherman bowed across the cold floor
and mumbled his offering. The mace-bearing hand moved slightly
and servants bore the blue-black thing to the kitchens. It bled
and stank. And there among the slime of its belly something shone.

A miracle! It was a gold ring set with diamonds, a priceless heirloom
fit only for a monarch, and so they praised all the gods and took it
to the king's innermost chamber while singing hymns of wonder.
But something was wrong. The king rose with a look of horror,

held the ring at arm's length. He clutched at his heart and fell. He knew this ring. It had been his most valuable possession, and a wise man had told him that unless he threw away whatever he held most dear, the gods would be envious of him and he would certainly be destroyed.

The poor fisherman knew nothing of such warnings and the story says no more about him. Think of him leaving, happy to be free, concerned only for his work to come. A god had rewarded him with a fateful gift. Giving it away had been everything.

THE UNIVERSAL KING

*Everyone without exception believes his own native customs, and the religion he
was brought up in, to be the best.*

Custom, says Pindar, is king of all.
When will we ever stop doing
exactly the same as everyone else?

Just like Darius the Persian King
we wake up, we get up, we get dressed,
and we go off to whatever we call work.

We might suggest to men from far lands
that their ancestral customs,
which are facts of living for them,
seem over time, or distance, merely *odd*.

*Would we dare to eat the dead bodies
of our own fathers and mothers?*

I am afraid, in several senses, that we already have.

*Would we burn people in ovens
and watch the smoke drift across the fields
in the harsh spring cold?*

That too, however you twist and squirm
there is no avoiding. People did it -
they were only obeying orders, so it may not have been their fault -
so the possibility of its happening again
is lodged in our thought, even though we are sure
that this time *we would refuse to do it.*

You see, concluded Darius, it is best
to do what others do, especially when
you arrive in a strange land

where you find the local customs
appalling, amusing, or simply wrong.
Any disrespect would be an error -

unhistorical we might say, lacking
in cultural flexibility, something

that can be explained from a distance,
or be laughed at, and ignored.

PREMONITION BEFORE BATTLE

You see those Persians at their dinner, and the army we left in camp by the river? In a
short time from now you will see but a few of all these men left alive......

Before Platea, the battle, that confusion where the army
of the Great King, though far outdistancing the enemy
in splendour and in strength, was nevertheless betrayed
by ill-advice and by poor disposition of our combined forces:

where after a hard struggle, in which our troops shone forth
in bravery and devotion to the service of His Great Highness,
they inexplicably failed to hold ground, and ran away,
pursued among the rocks, harried and cut down -

on the night before that disaster, we dined with some local nobles,
our allies during that time, safe within the city walls,
side by side Greek and Persian. And as the wine went round
and men laughed, I noticed my neighbour, a Persian, in tears.

The man to whom he was speaking, the Greek, seemed astonished,
because, as I overheard him, this man had prophesied
that the Persians here at the feast and those with the army
camped down by the river, would be dead very soon,

that nothing could be done to avert such a catastrophe,
it was the will of the gods. Alerting our generals with his fears
would be in vain, none of them would believe him in any case.
As they continued to drink, so his tears fell into the winebowl.

Men become sentimental like this when they are far from home,
tired of being on the move and fighting in strange lands,
when they drink too much. If it was indeed foresight,
the place strewn with dead, or whether I too was afraid,

my mind deadened , and later invented what I had heard,
so the vision became hindsight, I cannot be sure. The gods
will decide. It is the only the gods who can weigh the exact
                                                    difference
between the plain busy before battle, and later its emptiness.

CATS

When a house catches fire…nobody takes the least trouble to put it out, for it is only the cats that matter…

Wind rouses the dust in the empty street and pungent smoke
scrawls a black stroke on the air. A cooking fire has flared
a poor man's house. People are strolling idly past –

not filling buckets from the well, not forming a human chain,
not seeming bothered at all. The owner sits under a tree
brushing embers from his clothes, soot-faced, white-eyed,

shaken but relieved. Thank god, we have no cause for concern,
he assures an inquiring neighbour. The cats leapt from the window
and are sitting on a wall in the shade as the house burns out,

their glance tawny with flame. What a real stroke of luck,
they escaped unharmed. His seared hand blisters and swells,
screams from his children grow faint among the haze of smoke.

The holy ones yawn and stretch, then settle and close their eyes
and wait to be fed. It is fortunate indeed to be a holy one.
Passers-by utter thanks as they set off to morning prayers:

if you are a mere human, it is better to be destroyed.
If you have not yet been destroyed, then you haven't long to wait.
Praise to sudden sharp teeth, praise to the flurry of claws.

THE MESSENGER

Bare desert outcrop domed as a man's head
where thorns written on sand have blown clean,
hold this man's stare. Toiling along the road
he walks bowed in the heat and sweat rolls down

from his eyebrows over his face. Long ago
his skull was shaved and a message tattooed there
Start The Revolution, and he passed through
the Enemy's lines with his thick dark hair

hiding the secret. He can't remember now
whether they won or lost. With his hair silver-grey
thinning beneath his hood he can only go
on from village to town anonymously,

head-bent, shuffling, unspeaking. People grow tired
of reading his message when he does his party-piece
and he can't remove it now, only keep it covered –
three meaningless words raw as a sacrifice.

FRAGMENT OF ROAD

Along this ridge runs a section of ancient road,
an arrow fallen in grass. Resistance of the pull,
then thrust into the distance, like that paradox

of the ancients in which the scrabbling tortoise
outruns fleet Achilles: one part at a time,
the journey from A to B, an evening meal, sleep

and on to C the next day, outrunning the pace
of time, stone walls, fire-blackened, abandoned
fields, faint final spurts of channeled water,

footsteps, swirls of dust, endless talking.
Contours, crop-marks, ancient marginalia
might shake out the origin, the destination

of this lost limb, stretched out along the skyline
where the shade of outsmarted Achilles floats
like mist or dust in the game of catch-up.....

READING THE ANCIENTS

Settled in books, that was not their beginning.
Crouching in the noonday sun, dazzled,

and sweating, they clutched at their heads
and groaned in sickness, gazed at sunburnt

blistered legs, but found themselves on rocky
slopes, sweating, struggling on foot uphill

always higher. Finally came flights of steps,
library tables, crushed twisted strata

of paper, and men and women filing in
first gawping, then reaching with their hands

over the crumbled stones, in awe, enlivening
those shapes which shied off into uncertainty...

THE THIEF

There was a greedy king of Egypt, Rhampsinitus,
obsessed with wealth. The mason who built his strong-room
for his precious treasure was not paid as promised

so on his death-bed told his two sons the secret –
how to break in to the place. They paid regular visits
and carried off all they could, to even up the debt.

After a while of course it was obvious that someone
was filching the king's treasure, so he set up a man-trap,
and one of the brothers was caught in its metal jaws.

The other couldn't prise it open, so the one in the trap
knew what had to be done. Brother, he said,
to save yourself, you will have to cut off my head.

I am already a dead man, and this way nobody
will recognise me, and you will escape detection.
It must have been hard to do it, but his brother obeyed.

In the morning the king found only a headless body.
Rhampsinitus was puzzled, but then he ordered
that the corpse should be hung high on the palace wall

with a guard set over it, to see who came to mourn.
Of course the mother of the boys was horrified.
To leave her poor son's body swelling in the sun

was against her deepest beliefs. She knew what had happened,
and ordered her surviving son to retrieve the body
and bury it as was required. If not, she said,

she would go and throw herself upon the king's mercy
and tell him everything. The boy considered carefully
what he could do. He bought six donkeys in the market

and loaded them with bulging skins of wine,
then led them past the palace where his brother was hanging.
Secretly, he opened the wine-skins and shouted a lot:

My wine, my wine, help me, it's leaking out. The guards
ran up to help and ended up drinking most of it.
They were soon reeling about, then snoring in the shade.

The boy cut off their beards – it was a good joke –
retrieved his brother's body and gave it burial.
Everyone laughed at the soldiers, and the king was in a rage,

but after a while, like a proper king, he reflected
and had an announcement made throughout the country
that if the thief confessed, he would reward his skill

by marrying him to his most beautiful daughter,
provided he explained to the king exactly how
he had broken into the strong-room and stolen the money.

The young man thought that the king would keep his word
despite all evidence to the contrary. After all
the king was a greedy man, and broke his word

and was generally fairly stupid. But even so
he gave himself up at the palace and told the king
all that he wanted to know. The king saved face

and married the boy to the lovely princess.
Rhampsinitus could tell everyone that in Egypt,
though everyone was clever, as is well known,

his new son-in-law was the cleverest of all of them.

Biographical Note

Michael Vince, born in 1947, taught in Italy and Greece, where he lived and worked for many years. He now lives in London. He won an Eric Gregory Award in 1977, and has had two previous poetry collections published, by Caracanet, *The Orchard Well* (1978) and *In The New District* (1982), as well as the pamphlets *Mountain Epic and Dream* (1981) from Bran's Head and *Gaining Definition* (1986) from Robert L. Barth. His poems have appeared in magazines in the UK and the USA (Times Literary Supplement, London Review of Books, The Southern Review, La Fontana, Numbers, Verse, Poetry Nation Review) over the past forty years or more.

Other Mica Press Publications:

Graphologies by Phil Cohen with Jean McNeil 2014. £11.99
Paperback. ISBN 9781869848026. 86 pages 23.5 X 19.1 cms
with colour illustrations.

Archipelagos: poems by Leslie Bell 2012. £8.00.
Paperback - ISBN 9781869848019. 84 pages. 19.8 X 12.9 cms.

Lightning Source UK Ltd.
Milton Keynes UK
UKOW06f0731220215

246683UK00006B/14/P